Building Business with Agents and Distributors

A Practical and Profitable Approach to Selection, Management and Motivation

Gary Jennings

Building Business with Agents and Distributors

A Practical and Profitable Approach to Selection, Management and Motivation

Published by GJ International Ltd
www.gj-intl.com
PO Box 88, Bodmin. PL30 3WZ. UK

ISBN 978-0-9559333-0-1

Printed and bound in Great Britain by the MPG Books Group, Bodmin.

To Mom

I hope you are looking down from your cloud and that I make you proud

To Dad

For all that you have shown and taught me

But Mostly to Di

For everything and for you

. . . .

About the author

Gary Jennings is founder and managing director of GJ International Ltd, a business that specialises in working with companies to help them grow internationally.

His specialities include working in all areas of a business to orient it to become a global player, delivering key note speeches on issues surrounding internationalisation of companies, and developing, writing and delivering training programmes covering topics related to profitably growing international trade.

He has worked in international business development for the majority of his professional life and has a reputation for creativity and an intuitive understanding of what needs to be done to be successful.
Gary takes a practical perspective, as he says "I deliver what I do in my own company, therefore I know it works; I don't just tell people what I used to do".

His knowledge and real life experience gained from many years of working with agents and distributors throughout the world, and his unique, inclusive approach, has led him to be recognised and respected as one of the key resources in all aspects of building international business with agents and distributors.

He runs a free export resource website at www.exportingessentials.com. With a focus on profitably and effectively growing international business, he continues to be in demand for his international business development expertise from companies of all sizes throughout the world.

He is married to Diane and lives in Cornwall, UK with their two dogs, Archie and Hayley.

Contents   Page

Introduction

The relationship with your agent or distributor can make the difference to the growth and profit of your export business. This relationship is not just about interpersonal roles, it is also about understanding how your business affects their business, and theirs yours.

Effective management and motivation of your agent or distributor demands attention to detail; this book will introduce the principles of selecting, motivating and managing agents and distributors, and how to orient these partners in everyday business development, including:

- The roles of agents and distributors, how to profile the ideal partner, to appoint them, and how to maximise their profitability and growth through effective management and motivation.
- Understanding pitfalls and practical key skills needed to ensure continued success and growth.
- Developing frameworks for profiling, reporting and performing that can be applied and implemented within your own business.
- Looking towards business continuity and how to be prepared for changes.
- Trading issues that must be understood to ensure profitability.

This book is relevant to anyone who is responsible for the appointment and management of agents and distributors, for those who are new to international trade and also for those who are more experienced and wish to review their approach to the management of their agents and distributors.

This book is not developed from theory or textbook; all elements come from practical, current experience of working with agents and distributors within the international arena.

The main focus is on international agents and distributors, however the issues regarding selection, profiling, motivation and trading issues are relevant to most other types of international business partners including joint venture partners, licensees and franchisees.

Agents and Distributors

The choice between an agent and a distributor will depend on the market size, the type of product or service and the degree of control the supplier wants to exercise or is able to exercise in the market.

In its most simplistic form, the main advantage of working with an agent or distributor is that, if they are the right partner and managed correctly, they will be in the field finding and growing the supplier's business whilst they concentrate on growing business through other channels.

Selecting the right partner to be the in-market representative is vital to export success. Inappropriate partners and distribution structures can be very difficult to change once they are in the market.

A good relationship between the supplier (the principal) and their representative (the agent or distributor) is essential, which requires a strong, positive relationship based on open two-way communication, a genuine liking for each other, and high trust levels.

Every market is different, just as every company is different and there are no hard and fast rules that must be adhered to when working with agents and distributors; in many respects there is very little that is "black and white", it is more a case of working in "shades of grey". However, as experience in working with agents and distributors increases, the principal will understand what is needed in their own industry and in the marketplace. Principals who are flexible in their approach are usually the ones that are the most successful.

Although the terms "agent" and "distributor" are used interchangeably in the commercial world, there is a distinct legal difference between the two: in strict legal terms, an agent acts on behalf of another in assuming contractual obligations on the other's behalf. Whilst the function of a distributor is to re-sell goods bought from a supplier, an agent's function is to provide a service to the supplier, either introducing customers to the supplier, or concluding contracts on the supplier's behalf.

The simplest explanation of the difference between an agent and distributor is:

- An agent is a representative of the supplier, whereas a distributor is a customer of the supplier.
- A distributor takes title of your products, an agent does not (the supplier retains title until sold).
- An agent represents both products and services, a distributor represents products only (as they cannot take title of a service – if they deliver a service on behalf of the principal, then this is under a licensing agreement).

Depending on the circumstances of the particular case, the agent:
- may have authority to enter into contracts on behalf of the supplier;
- will act as the intermediary where the contract for the sale of the products or supply of services will be between the supplier and the customer; the supplier controlling the price and terms of supply to the customer;
- will generally have no liability under the contract made on the supplier's behalf;
- will not bear the risk of bad debts (the supplier will take the exposure); and
- will usually be remunerated by commission paid by the supplier.

Under a distributorship agreement, on the other hand, the distributor purchases goods from the supplier and resells them on his own account.

- The distributor has no authority to bind (i.e. incur contractual obligations on behalf of) the supplier.
- There are two separate contracts for the sale of the products: from the supplier to the distributor and from the distributor to the customer. The supplier has no direct contractual link with the customer and (depending on the territory concerned) the supplier may be prohibited from controlling the distributor's resale prices.
- The distributor bears the risk of customers' bad debts (and the supplier's risk of bad debts is channelled into one debtor, i.e., the distributor).
- The distributor is remunerated from the profit on the supply of the products to the customer.

Why Are Some Export Companies More Successful?

There are two key factors that differentiate a moderately successful company to a highly successful one; one is the business structure and the other is the principal's mindset.

The Business Structure

A question:

> Does your company sell through agents or distributors, or do you work with agents or distributors?

There is a subtle difference:

Those companies that sell through agents or distributors normally look at their business partners as secondary resources that have to fit in with their domestic business practices. The partner is usually expected to fit in and around the company, and any needs or requests they have may not be taken as a priority.

However, those companies that work <u>with</u> agents and distributors have a primary business model that orients their entire business to effectively work with agents or distributors to maximise all business opportunities; the "DNA" of their company is working <u>with</u> agents or distributors. The agent or distributor will find it easier to work with these companies, be more attuned to their offerings and usually be more prepared to promote them resulting in a greater success for both companies.

The Principal's Mindset

A key area in effectively managing and motivating the agent or distributor is the principal's mindset.

Even though the principal's objective and focus is to grow their own business, a reversal can work to a great advantage where the principal has the mindset that he works for the agent or distributor.

The principal must become an integral part of their partner's business. If the principal takes the perspective that he works for the agent or distributor's company, not vice versa, the principal will be better positioned to understand the issues and challenges faced and also what the agent or distributor needs to be successful. It will remove any barriers to growing the business as both parties will be on the same agenda.

As the business with an agent or distributor is based on mutual trust, this relationship is essentially personal and it is important that a principal meets with his/her prospective representative before appointing them. It is equally important to keep in close contact after the appointment. The success or failure of a representation agreement often depends on the personal relationship between the principal and the agent or distributor.

What are the Advantages and Disadvantages of using Agents and Distributors?

Advantages of using Commercial Agents and Distributors:

- They should already know the local market and can therefore offer a fast means of entry and a good source of market intelligence.
- They can communicate with customers in their own language and offer a convenient and 'user-friendly' means of responding to customers' requirements and problems.
- They often represent a range of complimentary products or services, which can be part of an integrated product range.
- They bear the cost of investigating the market.

Disadvantages of using Commercial Agents and Distributors:

- A common cause of friction is that a principal believes that his/her products are not being promoted as well as the other products being represented by the agent or distributor.
- As the market for a product develops, exclusivity can sometimes cause problems, especially if a geographical area has not been defined in the contract, or is larger than the agent or distributor can effectively service.
- Relying on an agent of distributor can sometimes tempt a principal to ignore the need to get to know the market and the customers.
- Much depends on the initial choice of agent or distributor, and if a chosen representative is not effective, it may take time for this to become apparent.
- If the agent or distributor represents a range of complimentary products or services, the principal is in competition for their time and attention.

In large markets (e.g. the USA), it may be necessary to appoint separate agents or distributors to service different states, territories or regions.

Key Differences between Agents and Distributors

Agent	Distributor
Sell products and services	Sell products only
A representative of the exporter – the exporter sells through an agent.	A customer of the exporter – the exporter sells to a distributor.
Not financially involved in the sale – the agent does not purchase the product from the principal.	Buys for own account, i.e. the distributor purchases the product from the principal and then sells to their customers.
Involved in facilitating import only if required.	Imports the product.
The agent works for the principal and is paid in an agreed way – normally sales commission, usually paid after the principal has been paid.	Marks up the supply price to cover additional in-market costs of ownership, distribution and invoicing/debt recovery.
Technically the customer is "owned" by the principal, but many agents have their own customer base.	The distributor has a strong relationship with customers.
Not normally responsible for after sales service.	Responsible for after sales service, including warranty and guarantee issues.
Distribution is not normally the responsibility of the agent. The principal is responsible for distribution costs incurred by their agent.	Distribution responsibility.
Exporter's name and contact details promoted on promotional material.	Usually has their name and contact details on promotional material.
No control of resale price.	Controls selling price.
Does not accept credit risk for principal.	Accepts credit risk of buyers.

Distributors Acting as Commercial Agents

The distinction between the activities of a distributor or an agent can become blurred.

An agent, in some cases, may hold a small stock of products for the principal to ensure fast supply to customers.

Similarly, a distributor may act as an agent with some customers, particularly with a very large order, where the customer receives a quotation from, negotiates with, and ultimately places the order directly with the principal. In a case such as this, the principal will usually reserve an agreed level of commission for the distributor throughout the entire process, and to allow for the distributor's obligations such as importation, logistics, installation, customer training, warranty, servicing and technical support.

The distributor would be involved throughout the entire sales process, to ensure that the customer is serviced effectively and efficiently, and that they remain an integral part of the business development.

Distributors Managing Sub-Agents

Due to the demographics of the market in some countries, distributors may appoint sub-agents to ensure they have full market coverage and can maximise on any potential sales opportunity.

Whereas this scenario can be difficult to manage from the principal's perspective, it does mean that the distributor has an effective communications channel with the marketplace.

Where the principal's distributor sells through sub-agents, the principal must ensure that any contract separates liabilities and is between the principal and distributor only. The principal/distributor agreement should specifically state that any sub-agents are contracted by the distributor not the principal, that the distributor takes responsibility for any contractual obligations with the sub-agents and the terms of the agreement between the principal and distributor are not transferable to the sub-agent.

Advantages and Disadvantages of an Agent

Advantages:

- Agents are independent, not a direct employee.
- Agents can be used for exports of large, one-off items, i.e. machinery.
- Agents can have very good market expertise, technical expertise and their own customer base.
- Agents may work on a fixed commission on all sales – the principals selling costs are known in advance and can be built into their pricing; the agent normally being paid after the buyer has paid the principal.
- The principal retains control over their branding as they are responsible for all marketing and promotion.
- Commercial agents are usually paid on results and the principal maintains the responsibility for customers and the control of items including pricing, promotion, delivery and after sales services.

Disadvantages

- The principal bears the cost of all deliveries.
- Stock is not usually held in the market; therefore the principal may have to supply a range of clients, which can result in a relatively complex distribution process.
- Depending on the market and service or product, the agent may not be involved in funding promotional activity and may not undertake marketing or promotion.
- The principal carries the credit risk on all transactions, but where the agent is paid after completion of the financial transaction, there is an incentive for the agent to follow up payment on the principal's behalf.

Advantages and Disadvantage of a Distributor

Advantages

- The principal usually has only one customer (the distributor), who may be responsible for credit risk on sales.
- The distributor holds stock.
- The distributor provides back-up service to clients.
- The distributor helps pay for and undertakes marketing and promotion of the product in the market.
- The distributor develops a customer base for the product.
- The distributor handles more of the in-market work.

Disadvantages

- The principal has minimal control in the selling process.
- The costs of selling through a distributor can make the product no longer competitive i.e. a distributor may add a high percentage mark-up to the product prior to it reaching the customer.
- The principal may not know their customers.
- As a distributor shares responsibility for marketing and promotion, the principal may not have full control over the branding.
- A distributor may represent multiple products, so their attention and time may well be divided and diluted.

The Six Steps to Selecting Your Agent or Distributor

Selecting the right agent or distributor to work with can be one of the most time consuming and difficult aspects of your international business.

The importance of finding the right partner will have a long term effect on sustainable business development. Get it right and the agent or distributor will be an extension of your business, get it wrong, and you will spend more time managing and motivating them, and trying to put things right, which will add immeasurable costs to your business and impact your growth and profitability.

The process can be broken down into six basic steps:

Step 1:

Decide exactly what you want the agent or distributor to do.

The obvious answer is to sell your product or service, but there are more issues that are just as, or sometimes more, important:

- Should they be able to market your products or service?
- Do they need to have specialist knowledge or skills?
- What contacts should they have or be able to approach?
- Do they have a customer service function?
- How will they handle accounts and reporting?

Thinking about and formalising these operational roles will not only help to shape the profile of the prospective partner, but will also give an insight into how they will fit within your business.

Step 2:

Create a profile of the ideal partner based on the operational roles.
The profile will be similar to a job specification, but cover their entire
business. It may be impossible to meet the profile completely; however it will
give an immediate understanding of the closest, and most relevant, fit to
your business and the marketplace.

Step 3:

Research and contact the prospective partners.
Ask for further company information and explain what you are trying to
achieve.

Step 4:

Visit them.
Get to know them, their set-up, who you would be in daily contact
with...and whether you like each other, each other's business and believe
that you can move forwards together.

Step 5:

Check out the legal requirements; contracts, bank and trade references and
financial reports.

Step 6:

If it all checks out, appoint them – but ensure that there is a documented
introductory strategy and plan, and milestones that they must meet within
the contract.

Step 1: The Key Roles of an Agent or Distributor

List the key operational roles your agent and distributor should be able to carry out. This checklist is not a financial business plan; it is a description of the functions you expect your ideal partner to perform.

Marketing

```



```

Sales

```



```

Target customers

```



```

Customer service

Technical or specialist support and service provision

Administration and reporting

Other

Step 2: Agent and Distributor Profiling

There are many key traits required of the ideal agent or distributor, and it is important to create a profile which includes all these traits. No two profiles will be identical, your ideal profile will be individual to your company, and perhaps even to the target market you intend to enter.

Developing an ideal profile for your agent or distributor is similar to developing a job description for an employee, but it is more in depth and has many more facets including their internal structure and the external marketplace. You cannot create an ideal profile without a full understanding of the marketplace you plan to enter and the external influences. The profile will help when interviewing prospective agents and distributors, to ensure that all elements and requirements are covered, enabling you to guage whether the agent or distributor is in control of their business, their future direction and growth.

The profile is broken down into six headings:

- The marketplace
- Company strengths
- Sales and marketing
- Staff and skills
- Product or service
- Fit with the principal

Each element is interrelated with all the others, and has a cause/effect relationship on the elements. Looking at the elements individually and also as a whole generates a holistic view of a potential partner.

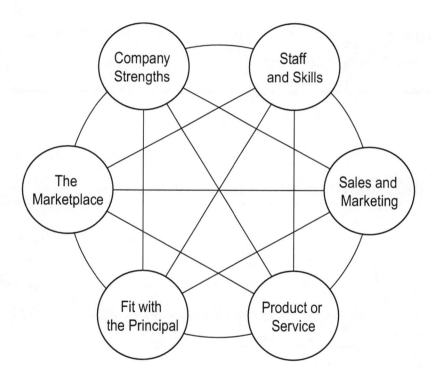

Agent, Distributor and Marketplace Profiling Checklist

The following checklist itemises the most important factors under each heading of the profile. When building up a profile, it is good practice to prioritise the essential factors (the needs) versus the ideal ones (the wants).

Mark each essential item with a tick and any ideal element with a "*". Add any specific comments or requirements.

The Marketplace

☐ Purchasing patterns.

```



```

☐ Product/service is already established and accepted or new niche must be built.

```



```

☐ The reputation of the agent/distributor in their marketplace.

```



```

☐ Competitive positioning.

```



```

☐ Political or legal influences.

```



```

☐ Registration demands.

```



```

☐ Other:

```



```

Company strengths

☐ Turn over, profit, growth key measure(s).

[ ]

☐ Ability to finance initial sales and marketing activities, and future growth.

[ ]

☐ Their position and standing with current and past customers, suppliers and the market.

[ ]

☐ Time established and company history.

[ ]

☐ Position in local business community.

[ ]

☐ Plans for the future – coherent and published business plan and growth plans.

[ ]

☐ Bank and trade (2) references.

[ ]

☐ Capacity to effectively represent you.

[ ]

☐ Facilities, IT systems.

☐ Usual way of working – how easy will it be to do business with them?

☐ Communications chain.

☐ Quality and/or regulatory systems, certification.

☐ Ability to support registration requirements.

```



```

☐ Membership of relevant trade associations.

```



```

☐ Other:

```



```

Sales and Marketing

☐ How they usually promote and sell – passive versus aggressive.

☐ Geographic coverage, satellite offices.

☐ Experience with target customers and target market.

☐ How they are positioned versus competitors.

☐ Number of sales and marketing staff.

☐ Contacts with influencers in the marketplace.

☐ Marketing plan.

☐ Produce local language promotional materials, manuals and website.

☐ Focus on customer satisfaction.

```


```

☐ Prepared to invest in advertising and training? How much over what timeframe?

```


```

☐ Provide market feedback to you on regular basis.

```


```

☐ Mechanism to produce quarterly and annual reports.

```


```

☐ Develop plan through setting objectives.

☐ Other:

Staff and Skills

☐ Capability.

```



```

☐ Skills and Expertise.

```



```

☐ Knowledge.

```



```

☐ Training and qualifications.

```



```

☐ Capacity.

[ ]

☐ Ongoing training and continuous professional development (CPD).

[ ]

☐ Departments: Sales, Marketing, Technical Support, Admin, Finance and Customer Service.

[ ]

☐ Motivation and incentives.

[ ]

☐ Empowered to make decisions.

☐ Teamwork and internal relations.

☐ Languages – proficiency.

☐ Competency of management team.

☐ Attitude: "can do" versus "may do".

☐ Internal culture and beliefs.

☐ Internal communications.

☐ Other:

Product or service

☐ Experience of product or service; selling, marketing, support.

☐ Complimentary / compatible product lines or services carried.

☐ Hold inventory and spares.

☐ Prepared to purchase demonstration stock or samples.

☐ Volatility of offerings over the past few years.

☐ Will they drop competing product lines?

☐ What percentage / turnover / profit, does each other product line represent?

☐ What percentage / turnover / profit will you represent?

☐ Which line incurs the highest internal / installation / support / warranty costs?

```



```

☐ Which line is the easiest to sell and which do the sales people prefer to sell?

```



```

☐ Which other principal gives them the best marketing support / materials / website / visits most?

```



```

☐ Will there be a dedicated product / service manager allocated? Who & experience?

```



```

☐ Do they receive customer complaints and how do they handle them?

☐ Other:

Fit with the principal

☐ Company culture.

☐ Communications.

☐ Ease of doing business with them.

☐ Knowledge.

☐ Drive and determination.

☐ Enthusiasm.

☐ Ethics and principles.

☐ Quality.

☐ Certification.

☐ Do you like them...

☐ Other:

Step 3: Identifying Potential Agents or Distributors

There are many sources of information to help identify agents or distributors in the target market; the initial steps can be made through desk-based research and networking with contacts. As the project progresses, costs will be incurred, which should be seen as an investment for the future growth of the principal's export business, not an operating expense:

On the internet, look at websites of companies who offer complimentary product or services; they may list current representatives, or may give details of some customers who have written testimonials.

Research competitor websites; they may also list similar information. A general search on internet search engines may also give references that can be researched.

Contact your in-country embassies and foreign trade desks in the target markets – and always visit them when you make a country visit; they are usually welcoming, like to know what is going on, and will help if they can.

Contact the trade desk of the foreign country embassy in your country. They usually have lists available, at a minimal cost, of agents or distributor companies, by sector, which could be a suitable partner.

Many countries have joint Chambers of Commerce e.g. the Turkish British Chamber of Commerce and Industry (www.tbcci.org) who can make contacts via the corresponding office overseas.

Work with government services who may be able to put you in contact with one of their trade advisors for their advice, or if they have any contacts.

If you have already traded in the marketplace, ask current customers, key opinion leaders or any other contacts in the country for recommendations or names of prospective partners.

Use a matchmaking website; contact suppliers of complimentary products to find out more about their company (internet matchmaking websites are normally free to use for buyers).

Read industry papers, journals or magazines, or sign up to email alerts. Companies and information sources are often mentioned in case studies.

Visit international or in-country exhibitions. Talk with various suppliers and exhibitors, and other delegates.

Network – very often an agent or distributor may find you – especially when you start to make general enquiries. If you ship products, perhaps your freight forwarder has contacts in that country too.

Place an advert in an industry or in-country journal or a comment on your own website, but be aware that this can encourage unsolicited responses from marketing organisations, approaches from unqualified prospects, and can also flag up your intentions to your competitors.

Work with third-party, independent export sales manager or export house. This can be more expensive, but can be of great value due to their country or sector specific knowledge and contacts. If using a third-party company, ensure that the project is accurately scoped and detailed in its requirements to ensure that the results meet your exact business needs.

Step 4: Meeting with your Prospective Agent or Distributor

Having made contact, arrange a trip to visit the prospective agents or distributors. Tell them that you are coming to evaluate them and that you will be seeing some of their competitors.

It is important that you go to their offices, meet their staff (if they are large enough) including sales, finance, marketing and service to ensure that they can meet your needs.

Spend time with them, and also if possible some social time (i.e. dinner together).

Remember this is a two-way interview; they are probably more experienced in the marketplace than you, but you may have more industry experience. Go through your ideal profile and see how they shape up to your needs.

One of the most important outcomes is that you like them, they like you, and you all feel as though you can work together. Remember though that the person who is hosting you may not be the same person who you will be your regular contact or representative; make sure you get to know all those who will be involved in your business.

Be aware of "distributor games": check out any claims or comments that are made about the market, the competition, other distributors or agents.

They will probably take you to meet a few customers – be aware that these will be their key customers or associates – not the market in general.

Discuss how they approach the market, their strategies, their strengths, their financial status, the age of the company, the growth of the company, their experience within the market sector and their influence within the marketplace.

Also make a couple of customer visits with them; obviously they will take you to meet their key accounts to make a positive impression, and discuss a high growth in future business. You will be able to see how comfortable they are in front of the customers and the type of relationships they are capable of building.

Do not make a decision "on the hoof" or be forced into a decision by the agent or distributor (they are sales guys after all) – always take time out and review and compare each meeting against the other – and take a second meeting if required. Once the decision is made, it is a difficult one to change, and can be one of the most detrimental to your sales in the marketplace.

Finally, until you have made a clear decision, do not leave the agent or distributor with brochures or flyers and information with which to review and test the market. By all means leave them with one set of brochures/flyers, but it could mean that by giving them half a dozen brochures and an instruction to test market feedback, you have appointed them by default as your authorised agent or distributor.

The 8C's

When meeting with any agent or distributor, either for the first time or as a follow-up evaluation, the 8C's should be used. The 8C's are:

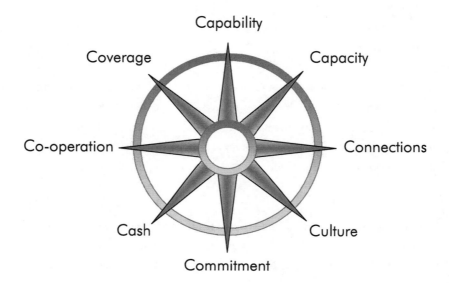

Keep the 8C's in mind when evaluating the agent or distributor's ongoing performance and assessing their overall suitability for future business growth.

It is also useful to form the basis for the first interview when meeting potential agents or distributors at an event (e.g. at an exhibition).

Capability: Do they have the skills, knowledge, understanding and ability to effectively represent your product or service? Have they the experience and have they worked in this field previously?

Capacity: Do they have the time, people and resources to establish and grow your part of the business?

Connections: Do they have experience in the field, and already have established contacts to approach?

Culture: Do you understand their culture, and do they understand yours? Not just the country culture, but that of each others business, the culture of the industry and the methodology of conducting business.

Commitment: Are they showing commitment to growing the business, to the marketplace, the motivation to move forwards and are they prepared to apportion resource and time to grow it?

Cash: Do they have the capital to invest in growth, in terms of time, people, equipment, marketing, training and understanding?

Co-operation: Are they prepared to co-operate at all levels both with you as the principal and the customer? Will they develop a business plan with you and report back regularly on progress made?

Coverage: Can they effectively cover the market or territory in terms of geography, and their internal capacity?

Step 5: The Legal Aspects

It is imperative that you understand the legal requirements, remembering that local laws can overrule any contractual agreements made. Use a legal professional with both international and in-country experience.

Do not rely on agreements that have been down-loaded from the internet as a "one-size-fits-all" contract; there will be industry and country specifics that must be understood and addressed.

Take up bank references on the prospective partner and obtain financial reports.

Ask for trade references and write to the contacts. If possible, talk with other principals that the agent or distributor represents; a five minute conversation will usually give all the information you need.

Step 6: Appointing Them

If everything is acceptable, then appoint them.

Ensure that there is a documented introductory strategy and plan, and milestones that they must meet written into the contract. Do not appoint them on a "let's see" basis; always have some form of contractual agreement, even if it is just for a three month period.

In the beginning, goals and milestones may be focused on marketing, customer contact and development activity. As the relationship grows, these may transition to be more revenue focused.

Decide on and implement a feedback and reporting structure, and use it consistently and at the timeframes agreed.

Motivating Agents and Distributors

How you motivate an agent or distributor is the key skill – get it right and you have a partner truly committed to long term profitable growth. Get it wrong, and it could mean being excluded from a marketplace for a very long time.

The biggest mistake that most principals make is to assume that their agent's or distributor's motivation is exactly the same, or similar, to their own; they forget that the agent or distributor may not have the same emotional attachment to the business, or the same reasons for driving their own business forwards.

Motivators will change over time, depending on personal situations and external influences, including:

- Culture – both the culture of the country and the company culture.
- Financial security - personal, company, or both.
- Size and strength of business – is the agent or distributor new to the market and very hungry for success at any cost, or have they built a strong business over time and may not be as aggressive in approaching the market, but have the position and contacts to be successful?
- Position within the marketplace – the reputation which the agent or distributor, or even the principal enjoys within the marketplace could be a greater factor in driving success.
- Dependants – this can be the employees and/or their families, any creditors (bank and trade) or commitments to customers.

Motivating the agent or distributor is the key to growing export business and is probably singularly the most important factor in meeting business growth objectives. Effectively motivating your distributor will give you the advantage over your competitors and will ensure they maintain focus, the results of which will be a sustainable growth.

You must first understand what motivates your agent or distributor as this will generate a greater sense of what is driving their business.

The main reason the agent or distributor is in business is to be profitable; it is not:
- to change the world,
- to be known as the person who introduced your product or service to their country,
- to be proud of the amount of business they generated for the principal.

Motivators can be specific to a particular industry, market, country or region. There are no hard and fast rules, but there are Three Pillars™ to Motivation and second tier principles that will drive the business moving forwards:

The Three Pillars™ to Motivation (see page 58) is what the agent or distributor needs to effectively do their job.

The second tier is what actually motivates them to do it.
This tier is supported by more personal elements (see page 61).

The result is that you are aligned with your agent or distributor, and both parties have a high level of motivation to move forwards.

The Three Pillars™ of Motivation

The First Pillar:
Make it easy to do business with me.

Throughout life, people will take the easy route. No one will really look to build and grow a business in a difficult way; therefore you need to make it easy for the agent or distributor to earn from you.

You are competing for the attention, focus and commitment of your agent or distributor - and the way for the partner to spend more man-hours in growing your business is by making it easier for the agent or distributor to make money.

It must be easier to trade with you than with any other company represented by the agent or distributor. You must provide all the "tools to do the job" to ensure success, which includes marketing, sales, technical and specialist information and access to any back-up and support that may be necessary in order to be successful.

The Second Pillar:
Make everything equate to a profit, value or saving.

Some principals may have a propensity to expect the agent or distributor to take their risk, to make minimal profits and absorb costs. They forget that the distributor is a company in their own right and is motivated by the same reason as the principal: to build business profitably.

The agent or distributor has a business to run, employees to consider, and commitments to meet. They cannot meet these obligations without making money, therefore you should ensure that any of the actions or activities of the agent or distributor equate to a profit, a value or a saving, whether directly or indirectly.

Obviously, not everything that the agent or distributor does on behalf of the principal will result in a receivable or invoice. However, focusing on their long-term revenue gain is the key.

If the agent or distributor can see that they will be profitable, they will take the action. If the agent or distributor can see that the principal is doing everything they can to help them maintain profitability, they will give their commitment.

The Third Pillar:
Make it easy to pay me.

One of the main, and in some cases unforeseen or unpredictable, cost that the agent, distributor or principal can incur is the cost of monetary transaction (bank charges).

Some principals demand payment by a certain route or from a specified bank. This may cause difficulties for the agent or distributor, and increase their costs. Your responsibility as the principal is to ensure that it is easy for the agent or distributor to pay you.

In orienting your business to be focused on The Three Pillars™ of Motivation, it will ensure that you are aligned to the export market, and that the agent or distributor can be more productive and effective when building their own business.

The Second Tier

The three pillars are supported by a series of second tier motivators which include:

Visit regularly.

If it is practical and economically viable, visit your agent or distributor regularly, especially at the start of the relationship. Give them the support they need in their marketplace. When asked, many principals cannot say what their agent or distributor is doing, or how they are doing; they have lost the personal contact. The majority of agent or distributor relationships break down due to lack of performance which can be attributed to the lack of time the principal has spent with the partner, perhaps meeting them when they first appoint them as their agent or distributor, and then expecting them to get on with the job in hand, without offering any support.

Get to know and understand the marketplace and culture.

In understanding the marketplace and culture, you will understand what is needed to be successful, become more aligned to the target market and ultimately give your partner the tools necessary to be successful.

Talk regularly and keep in contact.

It is very easy to use email as the primary form of communication, especially where time differences are great. Talking regularly will help to develop the relationship, and understanding. It is also a very quick and easy way to get a snapshot report of the business moving forwards.

Become a fit and boost to current business as a whole.

Ensure that you fit in with their business and that your products or services are a boost to their offerings.

Understand what the partner needs and wants.

This operates on various levels, from what they need and want to grow their business, to what they need and want in their personal life.

Pay commissions when requested.

One of the biggest demotivating factors for an agent or distributor is to be "held to ransom" over commission owed, where the reason for withholding the commission is not due to their actions.

Support business growth and after sales.

The old saying goes that "the sale is the start of the process, not the end of the process". Ensure that both your company and the agent or distributor can effectively support past clients whilst concentrating on current and new ones.

Honesty and consistency – keep promises

Ensure that there are no surprises for anyone by keeping your agent or distributor informed of any changes. Don't change an agreement unless it is fully discussed, explained and agreed.

The principal's mindset

As mentioned previously, think as though you work with the agent or distributor, not them work for you.

The Three Pillars™ and Second Tier Factors for Motivating Agents and Distributors

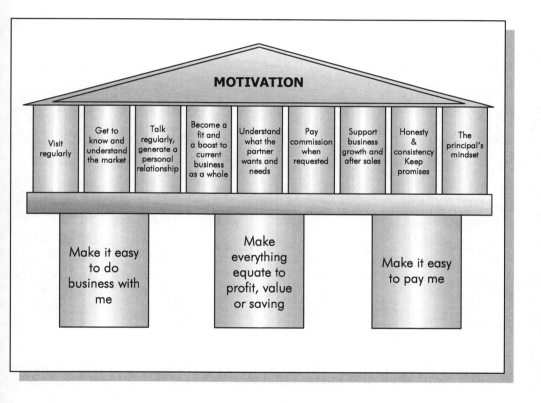

Motivation Checklist

Motivation is a key element to effectively managing agents and distributors.
Complete each section that applies to your business to record how you
intend to align your business and actions to ensure maximum motivation.

What must I do to make it easy to do business with me:

How can I develop everything to equal a profit, value, saving for my
distributor or agent:

What do I need to do to make it easy to pay me:

Visit regularly – plan:

Talk regularly – do not hide behind emails:

How I will get to know the marketplace:

How I will get to understand the culture:

How I plan to fit in with their business as a whole:

Other:

Developing the Relationship Further

As the principal–agent/distributor relationship develops, there are two key traits that must be adopted:

- Honesty
- Consistency

As the principal, you should be "straight" with your agent or distributor, and expect the same in return. It does not mean that you will disclose margins, profitability or maximum discounts, but you will be open and forthright with your partner. For example if you cannot do something or meet a deadline, you should say so; similarly if you can do something which would make a positive difference, you should say. Being open will develop a level of trust and understanding; both partners will know where they stand with each other at all times.

No Surprises

Consistency ensures there are no surprises for any of the partners. You should strive for consistency in business practice, pricing, terms and conditions, strategy and responses.

Being consistent will ultimately simplify business, and as discussed previously, if it is easy to do business with you, the agent or distributor will focus on you.

The agent or distributor will appreciate the positive effects of your honesty and consistency as the relationship builds, and ultimately it will develop into a binding partnership based on mutual respect, understanding and values.

Allocating Risk

In the early days of the relationship, the agent or distributor may expect the principal to take all risks and be very adaptable to their needs. This is just part of the sparring with an agent or distributor as they are trying to establish where the boundaries are. They know that if they can get the principal to accept some risk, or shipping charges, or finance charges, this could set the ground rules for the future relationship. If they can reduce their exposure to risk and limit their costs, they will — they are in business to make a profit, and they want to do that as simply as possible.

Many principals believe that the agent or distributor will always be trying to take advantage. Most agents and distributors in fact are there for the long-term. They do not look at making short-term gains in long-term losses. They are very aware of their personal reputation throughout the marketplace and with their peers. In most instances, a distributor may try to look for "the angle" to increase the chances of success in business; not to make a swift profit and then disappear.

Handling discount requests

If an agent or distributor asks for extra discounts, there are certain questions that you as the principal should know the answers to before making a decision:

- Why is the discount needed?
- What are the details of the order?
- What is the position and pricing of the competition?
- What products or services are the competitors offering? Are they comparable?
- When will the order be placed?
- What is the expected shipment of the goods or delivery of the service?
- What are the Incoterms (if applicable – products only)?
- What are the payment terms and payment mechanism?
- What level of commission is the agent or distributor expecting?
- What difference will it make to the market?
- Will any extra discount benchmark your pricing, product or service or devalue your offering?
- What represents completion of the contract?
- Are there any other factors (e.g. warranty, service provision) that will be required?

Sometimes discount requests are just a reaction or opinion of the agent or distributor, other times they are testing to see how far they can push the principal. It could be the customer who is trying to push for a better deal.

You should explain why the additional information is required so that the agent or distributor can accept that any decision is the right one for the marketplace and the future of the business partnership.

The Internet and the Role of Agents and Distributors

With the rise in popularity of the internet, many customers prefer to buy direct from the manufacturer believing that they will get the best deal open to them, or using the internet is more convenient for them. This has implications on the role of the agent or distributor as they can feel that the direct internet sales are undermining their position and hard work; an issue that has an impact on motivation and long term business development.

Internet trading is affected by competition laws and directives which vary by region, but often overwrite any contractual exclusivity granted to the agent or distributor; some legislation states that when an order is received through the internet it must be fulfilled by the principal regardless of whether any exclusive agreement is in place with the partner. Where these laws exist, they have been put in place to try to promote competition by reducing barriers to trade ensuring that all customers can try to find the best deal possible to them (whether the deal is more expensive in monetary terms or not, in the buyer's opinion, it is still their best option).

When formulating their internet strategy, many principals make a decision that the pricing on their websites will be their standard pricing without any discounts applied, and any extras (e.g. shipping) are charged at a specific rate. The standard pricing may include the costs of processing their internet orders directly which would not be applied if purchasing through an in-country agent or distributor.

If selling via the internet, you as the principal should ensure that your agent or distributor is fully aware of all elements of this direct trade. Many of the partners will be mistrustful and question their position, especially if the partner has an exclusive agreement. They may also question why you are prospecting for web-based sales when you have a competent and active business partner focused on increasing sales in their territory.

Many options exist in handling issues surrounding direct internet trade and keeping that agent or distributor motivated, including:

- Paying the agent or distributor a reduced commission or fixed fee on any internet sales into their territory.
- If the purchase requires some form of after-sales service, installation or warranty coverage, the agent or distributor can be paid a commission to cover the requirements.
- Ask the agent or distributor to forward up-to-date records of any business contacts or potential sales included in their regular reports. If a listed customer orders from the internet, this will be classed as a sale by the agent or distributor who will then earn their full commission.
- The internet business may have been set up to maximise opportunities in regions where your company does not have an agent or distributor. If a customer in the partner's territory finds the site through research or by accident, this is an additional opportunity to be capitalised upon which the agent or distributor can follow-up with to make additional sales.
- The details of any purchasers may be passed on to the agent or distributor (with the purchasers consent), so that the partner can contact them directly and therefore increase their customer base.
- The web pricing may be higher than the pricing charged by the agent or distributor and therefore their competitive position is protected anyway.

Be consistent and honest with your agent or distributor, ensuring that web based sales are not significantly detrimental to their position or own business. When developing your internet strategy, you must ensure that the issues surrounding the web sales and the agents and distributors are treated holistically, not as two individual businesses.

Paying and Transferring Commission

You as the principal should have your own rules regarding transferring commission to the agent or distributor, and you must be aware of money laundering legislation. It is recommended to only transfer commission to an account in the name of the company or the owner of the company, never to a third party, even a spouse.

Keep a separate commission account as appropriate to ensure funds are available when required, and maintain a paper-trail so that the partner can be shown the amounts and calculations if requested.

If there are outstanding balances owed by the distributor's or agent's customer, ascertain when these will be paid before making any commission payments. The last thing the supplier wants to do is to transfer commission if they are owed money. However if a customer or end user owes money, it can be against a country's legislation to withhold monies over a period of time, until payment is received. The principal can use commission transfer as a motivator, but not a threat.

Many principals ask whether they can use commissions owed to offset invoices. It may not be possible for a distributor or agent to use commission to pay for outstanding invoices as it may not show the correct movement of money with respect to importation of goods (balance of payments) in a particular market, culture or local laws.

The Profit Balance

As the export business develops, the profit balance between the principal and the agent or distributor can be a sensitive subject, and can be a balance that is sometimes hard to achieve for all parties to be totally content.

The higher the margin the agent or distributor can make will help to keep them motivated and focused on the principal, but too high a commission level can remove any hunger as they become more successful.

In some instances, the agent or distributor may seem to be making more profit than the principal, but if the principal exports to multiple countries, a higher number of smaller profits generate a higher base income stream.

There is also the issue of risk; the agent or distributor must sell the product or service to make their margin in their own territory – the agent or distributor carries the risk of no revenue, whereas the exporter may be generating revenue from a number of markets and thereby spreading risk. The agent or distributor can mitigate this risk by representing multiple principals, but the issue of focus and motivation is then more relevant and prevalent.

The final element is that of costs and frequency of sales. If the agent or distributor has to invest a high amount of time in order to close one sale, and incur a high level of costs, naturally they will be expecting an appropriately higher level of commission.

Conversely, if they are dealing in lower value, higher quantity sales that have a high repeat order frequency, then the commission level may be lower.

In establishing the level of commission, the principal should take into account the time factor from enquiry to order, to payment, costs and profit for the agent or distributor, industry norms and motivation of the agent or distributor.

One of the biggest issues that causes discontent amongst exporters is that they believe that the agent or distributor is receiving too much for the amount of work they do. In fact, many relationships have been terminated on this factor alone. This can be short-sighted as the agent or distributor would not be earning these levels if they had not increased business, and the probability is that the principal was happy when the business first started to grow. If the level of commission being earned becomes an issue, then it should be reviewed and discussed openly with the agent or distributor, but the principal must bear in mind that the act of opening this type of discussion could be a big demotivator to their partner.

Agreeing Targets and Reporting

In managing and motivating the agent or distributor, you as the principal must monitor the performance and effectiveness of the agent or distributor.

Three main tools are used:
- Agreed targets and forecasting
- Quarterly reports
- Annual reports

All three tools are used in conjunction with each other.

When forecasts are produced, it is very easy to think that all clients are potential customers, that there is a very high market potential; the forecast becoming a list of ideal outcomes.

The key is to ensure that the reports are realistic, taking into account internal and external influences such as:

Resources	Market potential
Capacity	Buying patterns
Capability	Competitive activity and reaction

One of the most challenging aspects of agent and distributor management is to gain accurate reports and forecasts, in a specified timeframe. The agency or distribution contract should include an annexe which lists expected outcomes (e.g. sales volume and revenue) and/or a requirement to produce reports on a monthly/quarterly and annual basis. Even though the agent or distributor may have agreed to this requirement, the reality of actually getting the information may be different.

Some agents or distributors will be more forthcoming, whereas others will culturally be more sceptical of giving a forecast and more protective of their in-country information; their concern being that you will have details of prospective sales targets and market intelligence that may be used as a pressure to perform as opposed to a joint plan moving forwards.

You will have to work hard to motivate the agent or distributor to complete the necessary reports and forecast. It cannot be assumed that they will automatically hand over the information. Key motivational points to take into account are:

1. Build the relationship. Keep your agent or distributor informed regarding their business, plans and objectives; this will generate an atmosphere of trust and information exchange.
2. As your agent or distributor trusts you more, and understands how the business is managed, they will be more forthcoming with information.
3. Make sure that your agent or distributor knows that the reports are not assumed to be an order commitment, but will be used for planning purposes.
4. Both sides should prepare the plan together, spending time to discuss and understand mutual goals and benefits.
5. The plan should take into account resources, capacity and capability of both your company and that of your agent or distributor, and the realisms of the marketplace, customers and competitors.
6. Your agent or distributor should also receive a copy of the plan once it is completed.
7. Ensure that the plan is built into your own scheduling so you can meet any obligations; the last thing any agent or distributor wants

to hear is that there is no capacity to meet an order for a product or service that has been included in their planning.

8. Keep your agent or distributor informed of any problems or issues and vice versa.

It is necessary that you as the principal produce a formalised forecast or business plan in conjunction with your agent or distributor. The monthly/quarterly and annual reports may be completed less formally, where you can build the report based on meetings, visits, conversations and even an informal discussion over dinner with your agent or distributor; the information is still as relevant, however the method of recording the detail is just a little less prescribed.

The following model performance agreement should be completed by you and your agent or distributor together, signed off by both parties and added as an annexe to the contract. The model reports are designed to be completed at regularly agreed intervals, either by your agent or distributor, or by you as the principal and fed back to them.

All the models are designed to be easily adapted to suit the business, sector, industry or market.

Model performance agreement

Business Forecast for .... (year), commencing .... (date)

Annexe .... to agency / distribution contract .... dated ....

Service / Product	Month	Volume (Qty, Days etc.)	Revenue (currency)	Quarterly target	
	1			Q1	
	2				
	3				
	4			Q2	
	5				
	6				
	7			Q3	
	8				
	9				
	10			Q4	
	11				
	12				
	Totals:				

Key activities

Target accounts
Product/service focus
Marketing activity
Support required
Other:

Frequency of review:

☐ Yearly	☐ Quarterly	☐ Monthly
☐ Other:		

Agreed by: ....

Principal   Agent

....

Sign   Sign

....

Date   Date

Model quarterly report

Period covered:	Date:
Completed by:	

Activities with key customers

Orders won	How

Orders lost	Reason for loss

Actions proposed to counter future losses	Timeframe

Support required from principal

Planned activity for next 3 months	Expected outcome

Competitive activity

Customer comments / feedback

Expected changes in market (tick)	
☐ Buying patterns	☐ Legal constraints
☐ Competitive activity	☐ Customer demographics
☐ Fund availability	☐ Cultural
☐ Governmental or political action	☐ Other:
Details:	

Forecast for next quarter

Service / Product	Key measure	Month	Target	Quarterly target	
		1		Q1	
		2			
		3			

Model annual report

Year covered:	Date:
Completed by:	

Orders / accounts won	Orders / accounts lost

Threats to business development

Planned strategy for next 12 months	Expected outcome

Support required to meet strategy

Planned activity for next 12 months, by Quarter
Q1:
Q2:
Q3:
Q4:

Expected reaction by competition

Customer comments / feedback

Expected changes in market	
☐ Buying patterns	☐ Legal constraints
☐ Competitive activity	☐ Customer demographics
☐ Fund availability	☐ Cultural
☐ Governmental or political action	☐ Other:
Details:	

☐ Forecast / business plan attached for next year

Agency and Distribution Contracts

An agreement can be either oral or written but either party has a right to require a signed document containing the provisions of the contract from the other party.

It is advisable for principals to draw up a written contract which outlines the exact details of the agreement to avoid as much trouble as possible if disputes arise or if the contract is terminated. The more detailed the contract is, the better it will be because there will be fewer issues to dispute. The contract can be used to enhance an agent's or distributor's obligations to their principal and can be used by the principal to better monitor the partner's performance.

All parties are advised to use a lawyer specialised in international commercial agreements due to the importance of the contract when engaging with the partner. It is also advisable to select a legal professional who has in-country experience as internal country laws can often supersede contractual jurisdiction and arbitration, even if agreed in the contract.

The most experienced lawyers usually start from the premise of "what happens if the relationship goes wrong", and work backwards from there to ensure minimal business disruption and cost, and to maximise continuity for the principal.

Model contracts are available, but these must be checked for in-country specifics; agreements and contracts must be formulated to protect both sides and to meet legislation including competition laws, restraint of trade laws, agency directives and distribution agreements.

Exclusive Contracts

The majority of agents or distributors will request exclusivity in their market or territory using the rationale that they are going to spend time and money developing the market and they need to be protected. They may also state that it is a market requirement and preferred by their customers.

Many exporters, especially those who are new to working with agents and distributors, may feel as though they have to grant exclusivity in order to be an attractive business proposition to the partner. They also think that by agreeing to exclusivity it will be the key motivator to the agent or distributor.

Before granting exclusivity, the partner's capacity and coverage should be evaluated. If the exclusive territory granted to the agent or distributor is too large for them to manage either due to the size of their company or the geography, the territory may need to be segregated into smaller key regions for a specific time period and reviewed at an agreed later date. This means that the territory can be targeted and managed more effectively thus enabling the partner to penetrate the market as opposed to spreading their efforts wide and thin.

Exclusivity can be an effective motivator, but it should be earned by the agent or distributor, not simply granted by the principal.

The principal may decide not to sell though any other partner, but use the goal of an exclusive contract as a future objective to keep the partner's motivation and attention.

The principal should explain that they have no intention of working with any other agent or distributor, but they need to see that the relationship is productive and manageable before making the commitment. The agent or distributor may not like the idea, but will usually understand the long term business potential and as the relationship progresses, trust and work with the principal.

Where competition directives and laws exist, there can be questions about exclusivity and whether it is non-competitive practice. The directives usually allow for exclusive agreements as they take the perspective that they are a necessary aspect of business development and providing and delivering products and service in the most efficient and cost effective way to end customers. However, as with all legal issues, relevant experts should be consulted before taking action.

Contract Checklist

Contracts should include certain standard elements as listed below. The list is not exhaustive and legal advice must be sought before discussing, negotiating or concluding any contract between the principal, agent or distributor.

- Identification of the parties.
- Definition of the contractual territory or group of customers and exclusivity.
- Duration of contract (including whether it is a fixed or an indefinite contract), notice period, and right to renewal/automatic renewal.
- Regulatory requirement (some countries require agents and distributors to be registered for example; others have regulatory demands of products and services).
- Agent / Distributor responsibilities, e.g. can the agent enter into contracts with third parties on behalf of the principal or should enquiries be passed on to the principal?; treat received information confidentially; keep the principal informed about the situation in the territory/with the

customer group; agent/distributor must use their best endeavour to promote the principal's product(s) or service(s) in the area/to the customer group.

- Principal's responsibilities, e.g. supply condition of sale to partner and clients; specify delivery details, order processing and quality of goods; set sales targets.
- The product(s) or service(s) covered by the contract, including after-sales services, guarantees, complaint procedures, conditions of sale and credit risk evaluations of customers.
- Intellectual property rights (patents, trade marks).
- Payment of commission.
- Indemnity/compensation.
- Transferability of obligations e.g. is it possible for either party to transfer or delegate its obligations to a third party?
- Restraint of trade clause (if required).
- Applicable law and jurisdiction.
- Modifications to the contract.
- Termination, cause and actions required upon termination.

Other elements that the principal may consider including in an agreement would cover performance and communication:

- Issue quarterly and annual reports.
- Produce sales forecasts on a rolling basis.
- Agreed targets.

Model agency and distribution contracts exist, but it is advisable to have the contract drawn up by a lawyer to ensure that all issues are covered correctly.

Terminating the Relationship

Terminating an agency or distribution agreement can be an extremely difficult and time consuming activity. The decision to terminate an agreement cannot be made lightly, and all ramifications on the business moving forwards should be assessed in detail. The termination will incur costs: legal, administration and incentives for the out-going agent or distributor, and potential loss of revenue.

The most important factor to consider when terminating the relationship is that of business continuity; whether the principal wishes to leave the market completely, or to transition to another partner, the effects on the business must be considered first.

Many principals only start to think of the implications of terminating the agent or distributor when a problem starts to arise. Experienced exporters however consider these issues before they start to enter the territory and well before they search for and appoint the agent or distributor. In fact, those companies who are oriented primarily to work with business partners in the export arena will have integrated these factors into their original plans and long term business strategy. This may seem a negative place to start, and the expectation is not that the agent or distributor will be fired, but it is to ensure that any effects on their business are understood and risks minimised before actions are taken.

Before terminating a contract with the agent or distributor, the principal must seek legal advice, refer to the agreement that is in place, and also review the obligations under in-country laws, directives and requirements.

The reason for terminating an agreement can be for many reasons including:

- The principal is withdrawing from the country.
- The principal wishes to have a direct presence in the marketplace.
- The agent or distributor is underperforming, or representing competitive products; in which case the principal will look to appoint another agent or distributor for the same territory.

Whatever the reason for termination, the focus must be on legal and contractual obligations, and business continuity (either in or out of the market).

Termination due to Performance

If the agent or distributor has not met the agreed performance targets, the principle should work with the agent or distributor to establish the reason. The shortfall may be due to market conditions, competitive activity, the product or service itself or lack of activity on the principal's or partner's part.

A plan should be put in place, with a specified timeframe, which is jointly agreed between the principal and the agent, or distributor, which will be closely managed and the results reviewed by the principal.

The principal should also discuss the possibility of termination if results do not improve, taking contractual notice periods and legal requirements of the country into account.

The Clean Water Principle™

The Clean Water Principle™ is a simple one: if you are going to make a decision or a change in direction, you should always ensure you have "clean water" to jump into not "muddied water". In other words, the actions taken will ensure that everything is clean and clear, with no uncertainties or loose ends (muddy water), to ensure minimal negative impact to any part of the business and maximum business continuity.

If it is deemed necessary to terminate an agent or distributor, the first step in the Clean Water Principle™ is to look at any current commitments to customers in the marketplace, and to work with the agent or distributor to gain maximum market knowledge with minimum business disruption.
For example, a distributor may carry stock to fulfil customer orders. If the agreement is terminated without taking the stock into account, the distributor may "dump" the stock into the marketplace at a minimal price which will negatively impact customers' pricing expectations for the future. It would become very difficult for the principal to grow the business in the short term, or attract another distributor.

When terminating an agreement, the principal should take the following into account:

- Outstanding quotation or tenders.
- Outstanding bid or performance bonds.
- Customer contracts currently in place or being negotiated.
- Warranty or guarantee obligations.
- Spare part requirements from current customers.
- Stock: purchased, demonstration and spare parts stock – buy and return value, whether returning to the principal or transferring to another agent or distributor.
- Marketing material.
- Customer database.
- Technical drawings.
- Sales activity.
- Quality and regulatory (QA/RA) records.
- Product registrations and certifications.
- Translated materials.
- Non-compete clause.
- A handover plan (if planning to work with another agent or distributor).
- The agent's or distributor's contract.

It is very important to establish incentives for the outgoing agent or distributor to ensure compliance and performance during the termination period.

In many cases, a series of objectives should be set, with timeframes, and an incentive attached to each. Once the objectives are completed satisfactorily, or the action implemented, the incentive can be paid. A final payment is usually made once all obligations are concluded correctly.

The process a principal will go through is shown in the following flowcharts.

Terminating an agent or distributor – decision to leave the marketplace

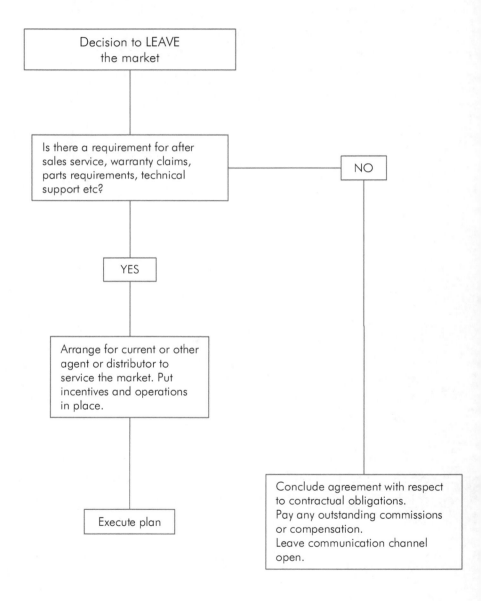

Decision to LEAVE
the market

Is there a requirement for after
sales service, warranty claims,
parts requirements, technical
support etc?

NO

YES

Arrange for current or other
agent or distributor to
service the market. Put
incentives and operations
in place.

Conclude agreement with respect
to contractual obligations.
Pay any outstanding commissions
or compensation.
Leave communication channel
open.

Execute plan

Terminating an agent or distributor – decision to stay in the marketplace

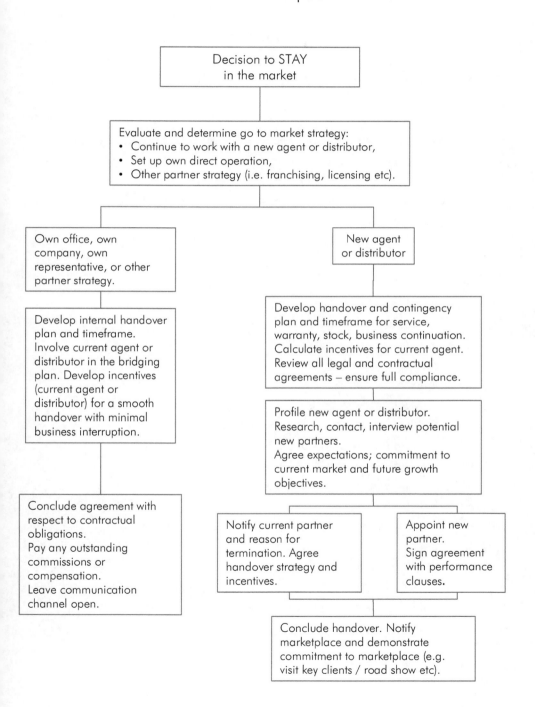

Decision to STAY
in the market

Evaluate and determine go to market strategy:
- Continue to work with a new agent or distributor,
- Set up own direct operation,
- Other partner strategy (i.e. franchising, licensing etc).

Own office, own company, own representative, or other partner strategy.

New agent or distributor

Develop internal handover plan and timeframe. Involve current agent or distributor in the bridging plan. Develop incentives (current agent or distributor) for a smooth handover with minimal business interruption.

Develop handover and contingency plan and timeframe for service, warranty, stock, business continuation. Calculate incentives for current agent. Review all legal and contractual agreements – ensure full compliance.

Profile new agent or distributor. Research, contact, interview potential new partners. Agree expectations; commitment to current market and future growth objectives.

Conclude agreement with respect to contractual obligations. Pay any outstanding commissions or compensation. Leave communication channel open.

Notify current partner and reason for termination. Agree handover strategy and incentives.

Appoint new partner. Sign agreement with performance clauses.

Conclude handover. Notify marketplace and demonstrate commitment to marketplace (e.g. visit key clients / road show etc).

Rules of Don't... ™

How not to motivate an agent or distributor

Motivating an agent and distributor takes time and effort to build the personal relationship; it is, however, easier to demotivate them.

Demotivators are not necessarily the opposite of motivators, they can be as simple as something the principal does not do.

The following Rules of Don't...™ are some of the key ways to demotivate an agent or distributor:

Don't...

- … try to control them.
- … mistrust them.
- … ignore their communications.
- … renege on agreements.
- … ignore their needs.
- … suddenly increase prices.
- … suddenly change terms and conditions.
- … set up dual distributors or agents without prior agreement.
- … suddenly change products or services.
- … stay away from the marketplace.
- … hide behind emails.
- … forget the importance of creating a personal relationship.
- … be inconsistent.
- … treat the agent or distributor like a sub-ordinate.
- … think they are making too much money or try to limit their earnings potential – if they are profitable, so are you !
- … break promises.

Quotations and Pro Forma Invoices

A quotation is normally issued to respond to a buyer's request for pricing. A Pro Forma is a quotation that is prepared in an invoice format.
In developing a quotation, the product or service must be clearly described; a foreign buyer may not be familiar with the product or service, the description may be more detailed on an export pro forma or quotation.

The following must be included in a quotation:
1. Seller's and buyer's name, address and VAT/tax registration number.
2. Date.
3. Buyer's reference number and seller's quotation/pro forma number.
4. List of requested product(s) or service(s), with a description of each line item.
5. Quantity of each item.
6. Price of each item, and extension (item price multiplied by quantity).
7. Cost of export packing (if not included in product price).
8. Any discounts.
9. Estimated shipment or courier costs (note: if a fixed price is not attained by the supplier from their shipping agent, any shipment or courier cost should always be stated as estimated).
10. Any taxes, VAT, duties or tariffs and relevant commodity codes.
11. Currency.
12. Payment term.
13. Validity.
14. Payment mechanism.
15. Incoterm (products only), including definition (e.g. Incoterms 2000).
16. Delivery point.
17. Total to be paid by the customer.

18. Gross and net shipping weights and dimensions when packed for export.
19. Estimated shipment lead time (products), or availability of commencement of service, from receipt of confirmed order.
20. Country of origin of goods.
21. Any particular conditions, for example:
    minimum order or shipment quantity (products),
    copyright or IPR (service) remains the ownership of the supplier until full payment is received.
22. Sellers bank and account details, including IBAN and BIC/SWIFT numbers.
23. Any restrictions such as: prices are subject to change without notice, the seller reserves the right to review pricing should there be a greater than 10% fluctuation in exchange rate, or E&OE (errors and omissions excluded).

Pro forma invoices can be used for payment purposes. They can also act as a model that the buyer can use when applying for import licenses, payment mechanisms (e.g. L/C) or arranging transfer of funds.
It is good practice to include a pro forma with any export quotation, whether or not one has been requested, as opposed to simply quoting a base price by email for example.

The principal should check any particular invoicing requirements that may be specified by the importing country when raising a final quotation or pro forma.

Export Pricing

Exporting can be more profitable than operating in a domestic market, but it can also be a drain on resources. Many exporters get drawn into the thrill, challenge and kudos of being successful overseas; however, the main factor to establish is whether exporting is profitable.

Being profitable is about setting the correct pricing, and also managing costs.

Whereas managing costs stems from the internal mechanisms within a company, developing the ideal price to enter a market and growing profitably is one of the most difficult areas for the exporter. This raises several questions:

- Should a pricing level be set that is extremely competitive to attract first time buyers, and then increase the pricing as sales increase, or should the pricing be set at the highest level and then discounted accordingly?
- In building the export pricing, should the seller use the pricing from their domestic market, and then increase it to cover extra costs or expenses?
- Or should the export pricing be established with a full understanding of all costs and implications?

The approach to building an export price will vary by market, by product or service and by sector.

The key to getting the pricing correct is to understand various interlinked elements within the business and marketplace including:

- The exporter's foreign market objective.
- Competitive strategy.
- Pricing strategies.
- Market demographics and competition.
- Cost structure.

Foreign Market Objectives

An important part of developing export pricing is to understand the company's foreign market objectives. For example, is exporting secondary to the company's current business and therefore does the company expect less from the market in terms of growth, revenue and profitability, or is exporting a key objective with key measurables such as profit, number of customers and sales?

Perhaps the exporter has a product or service line which has been superseded in the domestic market but has a potential elsewhere, or there is an excess stock, or service or manufacturing capability that can be utilised.

Whatever the objective, it will affect pricing considerations.

Competitive Strategies

There are three key competitive strategies: Cost leadership, differentiation and a focused or niche strategy.
Each strategy can be used to out-perform an industry rival.

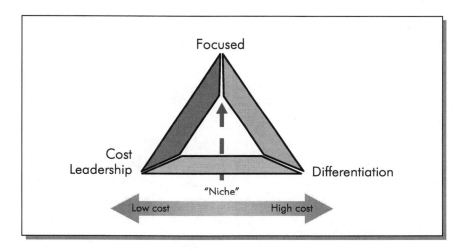

Cost Leadership: selling to a broad market segment at a low price through managing away cost.

Differentiation: offering a product or service which is perceived to be unique within the marketplace, to a narrower market segment.

Focused: providing the product or service to a particular niche (narrow) segment (e.g. geographic or consumer group) more effectively and efficiently than competitors who focus on one of the other two strategies.

Cost leadership and differentiation are at either end of the scale as far as cost is concerned; every uniqueness, whether product based or service focused, internal operations or delivery, incurs a cost to the supplier, hence differentiation is a higher cost strategy.

A focused strategy is used in conjunction with the other two: the supplier can either niche themselves as the cost leader – being the cheapest in the particular segment having managed out all possible costs from the supply and delivery chain, or hold a niche position through differentiation within a specific sector.

Many small companies or new exporters try to differentiate themselves and believe that they must sell at the lowest price due to a concern of market forces, competitive positions or not attracting customers. In trying to work at both ends of the scale, the supplier will be *stuck in the middle*. Differentiation has a value to the customer, and each differentiator carries a cost to the supplier. The supplier cannot afford to differentiate and compete on lowest cost as being *stuck in the middle* erodes profit and sustainability.

Most companies who decide to export do so as they believe their product or service is different to other companies, or that there is a marketplace that they can tap into. Due to the extra costs that are incurred through an export channel, it can be difficult to effectively compete on cost leadership (price) as local suppliers of the product or service have a lower cost base to begin with (they do not have the extra travel, packaging and shipping expenses). Therefore, the most effective strategy will normally be differentiation.

Differentiation can take on many aspects; it is not just the unique features of the product or service that can be the differentiator. The exporter can differentiate in areas such as quality, service, warranty and first to market. Again, the level of differentiation will attribute to the pricing level decisions the exporter has to make.

Pricing Strategies

Various pricing strategies are well documented, the most common of which are as follows:

Strategy	Description
Market skimming	High Price – competing either on uniqueness or quality. Unlikely to be much competition, maintaining this strategy will require additional support from the business (i.e. branding).
Sliding or reducing skim	Start with a high price - as competitors enter the market, gradually reduce the price. This is likely in situations where it is difficult to sustain a technological advantage or where costs are sensitive to economies of scale.
Market penetration	Low price is used to obtain volume sales and to attain market share. The price must not be so low that it indicates poor quality or unacceptable performance.
Floor pricing	Very low price is used to appeal to those who are very price conscious. Companies that can survive such low margins can do normally due to high turnover, low overheads or lower profit requirements. There is a strong requirement to closely monitor costs.
Competitor pricing	The price is set relative to a competitor's price; it can be higher or lower depending on the "competitive advantage" the exporter is promoting.
Cost-based pricing	All the strategies above imply that costs are managed to produce an adequate profit, in line with the pricing strategy which is adopted. This strategy identifies the costs and determines a price on a cost plus profit basis.

For each product or service offered, the seller must consider the implications of each pricing strategy. These implications include expected reaction of the market, the competitors and potential effects on current products and services, the business as a whole and in part (i.e. brands and brand equity, profitability).

Once a pricing strategy has been set and pricing announced, it is almost impossible to increase the price unless a re-brand or re-launch is undertaken, or new product or service features introduced.

Market Demographics and Competition

The exporter must understand the market, its potential and the supply chain. They should know what will be their own position in the market and be aware of the external influences on their potential customers:

- Are the customers willing and able to purchase?
- Will there be a high number of customers or is it a limited market?
- Are the customers located in key areas, or are they spread wide and thin?
- Do the customers have the necessary level of funds available to purchase, or will they need to finance?
- How do the customers usually take delivery of the product or service, and how often?
- What service levels will the customers expect?
- How do the competitors operate in the marketplace; what is their strategy, supply chain, customer base, position?
- Is the market open to a new entrant, or tending towards saturation with a high number of rivals?

The Cost Structure

Many exporters use a cost-plus system to develop their product or service export pricing, taking their domestic price, adding costs such as freight forwarding, commissions, customs charges and then a add profit margin. The effect of calculating a cost-plus price in this way can lead to escalating prices that are not competitive in the export arena. For example, the original UK customer price may already include profit margin and provision for functions such as customer service and support; a role that their agent or distributor will be responsible for.

The exporter should evaluate their costs, not necessarily down to the component cost level for a manufacturing company or evaluating a breakdown in hours for a service provider, but to ensure that any pricing calculation is developed from the base level cost, not a series of compound costs that also cover internal operations that are only applicable to the domestic market.

Building Export Pricing

There are two main elements to building the export pricing:

- Strategy
- Incremental costs

The strategic elements have been discussed earlier. The list of incremental costs will be individual to a particular product, service, or an individual market or order.

The main cost elements are listed below. Mark each cost that applies to your business/market/order and the forecast or actual cost. An exact cost that is not available should be marked as an assumed cost.

Cost element   Total cost

Product or service

Cost element	Total cost
Product unit cost .... multiplied by .... (qty for this order)	
Cost of undertaking service .... multiplied by .... (frequency)	
Adaptation costs of product or service to suit local market: Will the costs be amortised over this order, or a series of orders? Incremental cost per unit:	

Currency

Cost element	Total cost
Cost of receiving payment in foreign currency	
Costs of hedging, currency forward selling or stop order	

Payment mechanism type

Bank charges to cover receipt of payment (SWIFT or Draft)	
L/C or SBLC charges	
Confirmation charges	
Amendment charges or costs for presenting discrepant documents	
Payment term: .... Cost to cash flow / net present value (NPV)	
Export credit insurance	

Bonds

Bid bond	
Performance bond	
Bond cancellation costs	

Incoterms (products only)

Freight	
Insurance	
Duties and taxes	

Packing and documentation

Export packaging	
Labelling	

Legal fees

Contract or supply agreement review	
Notary costs	

Samples and demonstration stock

Cost of samples or demonstration stock amortised over this order or series of orders? Incremental cost per unit:	
Shipment of samples or demonstration stock	

Export and import documentation costs

Export certification: .... e.g. proof of export, movement certificates, certificates of origin	
Costs of certifying (notarising) documentation	
Pre-export inspection (products)	
Import license	
Import registration (products)	

Accreditations and approvals

Quality certification of product/ service after adaptation and translation	
Certification and/or registration in importing country	

Translation into local languages

Promotional material, literature, brochures, website, business cards etc	
Operators, service and technical manuals and software.	
Production of translated materials	
Shipping materials to distributor, agent or customer	

Time

Your time	
Other peoples' time	

Expenses

Travel	
Accommodation	
Subsistence	

Distributor or Agents Commission

Percentage or fixed cost? Rate	

Taxes and tariffs

Duty and/or tariff (both import and export)	
Taxes	

Other

Total:	

Pricing Terminology

When an agent, distributor or customer requests a quotation, they may use local terminology to specify the quotation type. The following list clarifies some of the more common terms that can be encountered in the export arena:

Term	Meaning
Net	The ex-works price, packed for export.
Gross	The ex-works price, packed for export, including agents or distributors commission.
Distributor net	Same as net, i.e. commission not included.
Net net	Same as net.
Customer net	Same as gross.
CIF (pronounced "siff")	The price delivered to the customs border (frontier) in the purchaser's country.
Netto	Same as net.
Brutto	Same as gross.
Customer price	End user price, including agents or distributors commission. Can include shipment, as CIF price, or one of the Delivered Incoterms – must be clarified by the exporter.
FOB (pronounced "fobb")	The price delivered to the customs border (frontier) in the seller's country.
ARP	Average realisable price.
ASP	Average selling price.

Incoterms 2000
INternational COmmercial TERMS

Incoterms are a series of internationally recognised standard trade definitions used in international sales contracts for goods and products.

The trade terms define the obligations and responsibilities of the exporter (seller) and the importer (buyer) for the delivery of goods, and how risks and costs are divided.
The terms relate to the trade terms in a contract of sale between buyer and seller and do not deal with the contract of carriage or payment mechanism.

The terms state the point at which the goods are "delivered", meaning the point at which the obligations for carriage, risk and costs transfer from the seller to the buyer.

The terms are published by the International Chamber of Commerce (ICC) and are regularly updated to reflect changes in international trade. It is recommended that the buyer and seller are both familiar with, and understand, the terms correctly. The latest iteration is Incoterms 2000 and full copies are available from the ICC on-line book store or from a local Chamber of Commerce.

Under Incoterms 2000, the terms are grouped into E, F, C or D terms designated by the first letter of the term. The list on the following pages gives an overview of each term; for a complete explanation of the full responsibilities, the ICC publications must be reviewed.

The "E" term: Departure

EXW   (... named place)
Ex Works

EXW means that the goods are classed as being delivered at the seller's premises or another named place (i.e. factory, warehouse etc).
The buyer is responsible for loading the goods, export clearance and all subsequent costs and risks.

The "F" terms: Main Carriage Unpaid

FCA   (... named place)
Free Carrier

FCA means that the goods are delivered when the seller has handed over the goods, cleared for export, to the buyers named carrier.
The carrier is any person who performs transport by rail, road, air, sea, inland waterway or by any combination, whether they perform the transport themselves or procure the transport services.
If delivery occurs at the seller's premises, the seller is responsible for loading; if the delivery is at any other place, the buyer has the responsibility.
If the buyer instructs the seller to deliver the goods to a person (i.e. freight forwarder) who is not a "carrier", the seller has met his obligation when they deliver to that person.
The buyer is responsible for the main carriage/freight, cargo insurance and other costs and risks.

FAS   (... named port of shipment)
Free Alongside Ship

FAS means that the seller has delivered when the goods are placed alongside the vessel at the named port of shipment. The seller is responsible for clearing the goods for export.
The buyer is responsible for the loading fee, main carriage/freight, cargo insurance, and other costs and risks.

FOB   (... named port of shipment)
Free on Board

FOB means that the seller has delivered the goods when they pass the ship's rail at the named port of shipment.
The seller is responsible to clear goods for exports, with the buyer responsible for the main carriage/freight, cargo insurance and other costs and risks to the goods from that point.

The "C" terms: Main Carriage Paid

CFR   (... named port of destination)
Cost and Freight

CFR means that the seller has delivered the goods when they pass the ship's rail at the named port of destination.
The seller clears the goods for export, and pays cost and freight to the named port of destination. The buyer is responsible for the cargo insurance, takes the risks of loss or damage and all other costs and risks after delivery.

CIF   (… named port of destination)
Cost, Insurance and Freight

CIF means that the seller has the same obligations as CFR, but must also arrange and pay for insurance to the point the goods are delivered. All risks then transfer to the buyer who is also responsible for the import customs clearance and other costs and risks.

CPT   (… named place of destination)
Carriage Paid to

CPT means that the seller is responsible for delivering the goods to the carrier, and the costs of carriage to the named place of destination.
The buyer is responsible for cargo insurance, import customs clearance, payment of customs duties and taxes, and other costs and risks AFTER delivery to the carrier.
If more than one carrier is used for delivery to the agreed destination, the risk passes to the buyer when the goods have been delivered to the first carrier.

CIP   (… named place of destination)
Carriage and Insurance Paid To

CIP means that the seller has the same obligations as CPT, but must also arrange and pay for insurance to the point at which the goods are delivered.
The buyer is responsible for import customs clearance, payment of customs duties and taxes, and other costs and risks.
If more than one carrier is used for delivery to the agreed destination, the risk passes to the buyer when the goods have been delivered to the first carrier.

The "D" terms: Arrival

DAF   (... named place)
Delivered At Frontier

DAF means that the seller has delivered the goods when they are placed at the disposal of the buyer on the arriving means of transport, having been cleared for export.
The buyer is responsible for unloading, import customs clearance, payment of customs duties and taxes, and other costs and risks.
The Frontier can be any frontier, including the country of export. Therefore the frontier must be specified and defined by name and place.

DES   (... named port of destination)
Delivered Ex Ship

DES means that the seller has delivered the goods when they are placed at the disposal of the buyer on the arriving vessel, having been cleared for export.
The buyer is responsible for unloading, import customs clearance, payment of customs duties and taxes and other costs and risks.

DEQ   (... named port of destination)
Delivered Ex Quay

DEQ means that the seller has delivered the goods when they are placed at the disposal of the buyer on the quay of the named port of destination, not cleared for import. The seller is responsible for the cost and risks to the port of destination.
The buyer is responsible for import customs clearance, payment of customs duties and taxes and other costs and risks.

DDU   (... named place of destination)
Delivered Duty Unpaid

DDU means that the seller has delivered the goods when they are placed at the disposal of the buyer at the named place of destination, not cleared for import and not unloaded. The seller is responsible for the costs and the risks of the delivery to the place of destination. The buyer is responsible for import customs clearance, payment of customs duties and taxes and other costs and risks.

DDP   (... named place of destination)
Delivered Duty Paid

DDP means that the seller has the same obligations as DDU, but is responsible for clearing for import (but not unloading) at the place of destination. The seller is responsible for the costs and the risks of the delivery, including any import customs clearance, payment of customs duties and taxes and other costs and risks, to the place of destination.

The following table shows the obligations and responsibility for charges of the importer and exporter.

Incoterms 2000: Obligations and responsibility for charges of importer (buyer) and exporter (seller)

Service	EXW	FCA	FAS	FOB	CFR	CIF	CPT	CIP	DAF	DES	DEQ	DDU	DDU
Warehouse services	Seller	Seller	Seller	Seller	Seller	Seller	Seller	Seller	Seller	Seller	Seller	Seller	Seller
Export packing	Seller	Seller	Seller	Seller	Seller	Seller	Seller	Seller	Seller	Seller	Seller	Seller	Seller
Loading at point of origin	Buyer	Seller	Seller	Seller	Seller	Seller	Seller	Seller	Seller	Seller	Seller	Seller	Seller
Inland freight	Buyer	Seller	Seller	Seller	Seller	Seller	Seller	Seller	Seller	Seller	Seller	Seller	Seller
Port receiving charges	Buyer	Seller	Seller	Seller	Seller	Seller	Seller	Seller	Seller	Seller	Seller	Seller	Seller
Forwarder fees	Buyer	Seller	Seller	Seller	Seller	Seller	Seller	Seller	Seller	Seller	Seller	Seller	Seller
Ocean / air freight	Buyer	Buyer	Buyer	Buyer	Seller	Seller	Seller	Seller	Seller	Seller	Seller	Seller	Seller
Charges in foreign ports / airports	Buyer	Buyer	Buyer	Buyer	Buyer	Buyer	Buyer	Buyer	Buyer	Buyer	Seller	Seller	Seller
Customs clearance	Buyer	Buyer	Buyer	Buyer	Buyer	Buyer	Buyer	Buyer	Buyer	Buyer	Buyer	Buyer	Seller
Customs duties	Buyer	Buyer	Buyer	Buyer	Buyer	Buyer	Buyer	Buyer	Buyer	Buyer	Buyer	Buyer	Seller
Delivery charges to final destination	Buyer	Buyer	Buyer	Buyer	Buyer	Buyer	Buyer	Buyer	Buyer	Buyer	Buyer	Seller	Seller

Using Incoterms

The following should be considered when selecting the right Incoterm for the import/export contract:

- Economic and political climate of the import/export market
- Payment mechanism and term/ usance
- Relationship between the buyer and seller
- Mode of transport
- Carriage of goods
- Cost
- Risk

When stating an Incoterm in a contract or quotation, the year of amendment must be stated in full to ensure that there is no confusion over the meaning and relevance: e.g. ....*price is Ex Works (Incoterms 2000)*.

A proof of export should be sought by the seller to meet with customs requirements in the seller's country, especially when using EXW terms. A Bill of Lading or delivery note is not always accepted as proof of export.

When selecting an Incoterm, the payment mechanism and terms (usance) being used or negotiated should be taken into consideration, with relation to the point where risk and title of goods passes from the seller to the buyer. For example, you would not expect to use Ex Works (EXW Incoterms 2000) where the seller's obligation is to their "factory door", with a payment term of "on receipt", meaning that the seller would not get paid until the goods are received on site in the destination country. In this instance, if the goods do not arrive for any reason which is outside the seller's control, he accrues all risks and will not receive payment.

Similarly the shipment type must be considered: if using any of the C or D terms, where main carriage is paid and/or up to the point of arrival, the seller would want to specify the method of shipment and probably the name of the carrier – the seller would not usually agree to use the buyer's nominated forwarder or carrier as the seller is the one who is responsible for the carriage and the risk, and should remain in control of the shipment.

Roles and responsibilities can be altered or changed providing that a written agreement is in place between the seller and the buyer.

RECOMMENDED MODES OF TRANSPORTATION		
Mode	Term	
Any Mode of Transport Including Multimodal	EXW	Ex Works (…Named Place)
	FCA	Free Carrier (…Named Place)
	CPT	Carriage Paid To (…Named Place)
	CIP	Carriage and Insurance Paid To (…Named Place of Destination)
	DAF	Delivered at Frontier (…Named Place)
	DDU	Delivered Duty Unpaid (…Named Place of Destination)
	DDP	Delivered Duty Paid (…Named Place of Destination)
Air	FCA	Free Carrier (…Named Place)
Rail	FCA	Free Carrier (…Named Place)
Ocean	FAS	Free Alongside Ship (…Named Port of Shipment)
	FOB	Free on Board (…Named Port of Shipment)
	CFR	Cost and Freight (…Named Port of Destination)
	CIF	Cost, Insurance and Freight (…Named Port of Destination)
	DES	Delivery Ex Ship (…Named Port of Destination)
	DEQ	Delivered Ex Quay (…Named Port of Destination)

Incoterms only relate to trade terms in the contract of sale between the buyer and seller and do not deal with the contract for carriage.

The roles and responsibilities listed can be altered or changed as long as there is an agreement in place between the buyer and seller.

Only two Incoterms specify when insurance is to be bought and issued: CIP and CIF.

When using an Incoterm in a contract or quotation, the year of amendment must also be stated in full e.g.:   ...*Price is Ex Works (EXW Incoterms 2000)*

When using CIF, you should specify *YOUR* nominated freight forwarder

If using FCA with a payment (usance) term, the named place is the cargo receipt e.g ...*Price is Free Carrier (FCA Incoterms 2000). Payment: 60 days from Cargo Receipt*

International Payment Mechanisms

To be truly successful, the exporter must master the usage of international payment mechanisms.

A deal is not completed nor the process concluded until you get paid; not on shipment, not fulfilling the service as agreed, not placing the order, not finalising the negotiation...the entire process is only completed when you get paid.

International credit, international finance, getting paid – it can be given any preferred title, but it is the underlying primary consideration in any business transaction.

Getting paid for providing goods or services is critical for any business. However, getting paid for an international transaction (also commonly known as "export receivables") can be a very different experience from securing payment on business in the domestic market due to the number of extra factors that can influence the process.

Many companies have developed their own policies and procedures, to run an international payment system, that tend to snowball into complexity. In establishing the payment policy, the principal should be able to answer one simple question: have I made it easy to be paid? The international payment mechanism can maintain the agent's and distributor's attention, focus and motivation, and the customer's commitment to buy.

Note that none of the methods outlined will completely eliminate payment risks associated with international trade; the preferred payment option should be selected with care and risks hedged utilising appropriate credit insurance and credit checks.

The main factor in considering how an exporter expects to be paid for a transaction is the potential risk that they and their customer are willing to face between them; there are always two sides to any situation. There are different types of risk that the exporter will face.

Before issuing quotations or commencing negotiations, the buyer and seller should consider where they will be comfortable in placing themselves on the diagram below, and what the other party will expect or need.

Payment Risk Ladder

Exporter:	Least Secure →	Less Secure →	More Secure →	Most Secure
Importer:	Most Secure	← More Secure	← Less Secure	← Least Secure
Payment mechanism:	Open Account	Bills for Collection	Documentary Credits	Advance Payment

The most common payment mechanisms are discussed below. Full information regarding costs and practice can be sourced from your bank.

Open Account

This is the least secure method of trading for the exporter, but the most attractive to buyers. Goods are shipped and documents are remitted directly to the buyer, with a request for payment at the appropriate time (immediately, or at an agreed future date). An exporter has little or no control over the process, except for imposing future trading terms and conditions on the buyer. Clearly, this payment method is the most advantageous for the buyer, in cash flow and cost terms. As a consequence, Open Account trading should only be considered when an exporter is sufficiently confident that payment will be received.

It should be noted that in certain markets, buyers will expect Open Account terms. The exporter should be aware of the local practices, as opposed to the quoted or negotiated payment term; the seller's quotation may expressly state that payment terms are 30 days, but the in-country norm could be 360 days. This period can be driven by cultural norms or governmental payments systems filtering through the supply chain. If there is no other option, factoring of forfeiting could be an option to manage cash flows. The financial risk can often be mitigated by obtaining a credit insurance policy that provides reimbursement up to an agreed financial limit to cover the potential insolvency of a customer.

Advance Payment

The most secure method of trading for exporters and, consequently, the least attractive for buyers.
Advance Payment is exactly what it says; the buyer pays for the products or services, in full, in advance. The advance payment can be required before shipment of the product or delivery of the service, or in advance of manufacture or developing the service.

Be aware, many buyers are adept at managing their cash flow. For example, a manufacturer may stipulate advance payment before shipment. The goods are produced in the agreed timeframe but the buyer may not transfer payment immediately, which means that the manufacturer cannot ship. This impacts the seller's cash flow due to the investment in materials, time and manufacturing capacity. The finished products can only be shipped once payment is received. In such a case, one option is to opt for a mix of advanced terms, for example 50% to begin manufacture, 40% at shipment and 10% at 30 days open account or as Cash against Documents (CAD).

As one might imagine, having covered the two extremes on the Payment Risk Ladder, commercial decisions have to be made and this usually results in selecting one of the middle rungs of the ladder. This is where banking products such as Bills for Collection and Letters of Credit come into play.

Bills for Collection

More secure for an exporter than Open Account trading, as the exporter's documentation is sent from a UK bank to the buyer's bank. This invariably occurs after shipment and contains specific instructions that must be obeyed. Should the buyer fail to comply, the exporter does, in certain circumstances, retain title to the goods, which may be recoverable. The buyer's bank will act on instructions provided by the exporter, via their own bank, and often provides a useful communication route through which disputes are resolved.

The Bills for Collection process is governed by a set of rules, published by the International Chamber of Commerce (ICC) called "Uniform Rules for Collections" document number 522 (URC522). Over 90% of the world's banks adhere to this document – however, the exporter should check with their own bank to ensure that the receiving bank does comply.

Be aware that in some developing countries the banking system may not fully follow URC522 rules; it is possible for documents to be released by a bank and goods cleared from customs without payment being transferred.

There are two types of Bill for Collection, which are usually determined by the payment terms agreed within the commercial contract. Different benefits are afforded to exporters by each and they are covered separately as follows:

Cash Against Documents (CAD) or Documents against Payment (D/P)

Usually used where payment is expected from the buyer immediately, otherwise known as "at sight".

The buyer's bank is instructed to release the exporter's goods only when payment has been made. Where goods have been shipped by sea freight, covered by a full set of Bills of Lading, title is retained by the exporter until these documents are properly released to the buyer. Unfortunately, for airfreight items, unless the goods are consigned to the buyer's bank* no such control is available under an Air Waybill or Air Consignment Note, as these documents are merely "movement certificates" rather than "documents of title". Similarly there is no such control available for road or rail transport.
 * Under URC522, goods should not be consigned to a bank without prior approval.

Using CAD is a cost effective method for both the seller and the buyer, and also sends a message of trust to the buyer, which motivates and keeps business simple.

Documents against Acceptance (D/A) or Term or Usance Drafts

Used where a credit period (e.g. 30/60/90 days - 'sight of document' or from 'date of shipment') has been agreed between the exporter and buyer. The buyer is able to collect the documents against their undertaking to pay on an agreed date in the future, rather than immediate payment. The exporter's documents are usually accompanied by a "Draft" or "Bill of

Exchange" which looks something like a cheque, but is payable by (drawn on) the buyer.

When a buyer (drawee) agrees to pay on a certain date, they sign (accept) the draft. It is against this acceptance that documents are released to the buyer. Up until the point of acceptance, the exporter may retain control of the goods, as in the D/P scenario above. However, after acceptance, the exporter is financially exposed until the buyer actually initiates payment through their bank.

Bills for Collection are a cost-effective method of evidencing a transaction for buyers, where documents are handled (and reported) via the banking system.

Avalised Term Drafts

The word "aval" in French means endorsement. A term or Usance draft accepted by the importer does not guarantee payment on maturity. The exporter may arrange to have the accepted draft to be 'avalised' by the importer's bank; the bank adds its endorsement as guarantee of payment. The 'avalised' term draft can be readily discounted, thus providing the exporter with immediate funds.

If the importer agrees to an avalised draft, it should be noted that the value of the draft is normally secured against funds in the importers account, therefore effectively blocking the draft amount and impacting the buyer's cash flow.

Letters of Credit (L/Cs),
or Documentary Credits (D/Cs)

What is a L/C?

A L/C is a bank-to-bank commitment of payment in favour of an exporter, guaranteeing that payment will be made against certain documents that, on presentation, are found to be in compliance with terms set by the buyer. Like Bills for Collections, L/Cs are governed by a set of rules from the ICC. In this case, the document is called; "Uniform Customs and Practice" and the latest version is document number 600. In short, it is known as UCP600 and over 90% of the world's banks adhere to this document.

This is an area in which financial terminology and acronyms are virulent. The more commonly used terms are:

Irrevocable: The terms and conditions within a L/C cannot be changed without the express agreement of the exporter (the beneficiary). Revocable L/Cs are very unusual, as the conditions can be changed unilaterally by the buyer (the applicant), which is rarely acceptable to an exporter.

Unconfirmed: The payment commitment within the L/C is provided by the buyer's (Issuing) Bank.

Confirmed: If an exporter has any concerns about the circumstances which may prevent payment being made from either the Issuing Bank or buyer's Country, the adding of "Confirmation" moves the bank or country risk issues to the bank which adds it's confirmation (the Advising bank) and notifies the L/C to the exporter. The price of such a confirmation will obviously depend upon the level of perceived risks to be covered. Banks can often provide indicative pricing for confirmations prior to the arrival of the L/C, so that costs can be estimated. Confirmation is not always required; before the seller demands a Confirmed and Irrevocable Letter of Credit as their payment term, they should consult with their bank who can advise on whether the destination country and related risk requires the L/C to be confirmed.

Pitfalls with L/Cs

Open ended L/Cs

Payment terms on an L/C can be almost any that the applicant wishes to enforce, which can include such vague terms as payment after installation, payment after commissioning, payment after successful completion of a service or payment after acceptance of installed products.

If the seller has to accept an L/C where the payment date is vague and/or dependent on the action of a third party, an amendment should be requested which will state the deadline in which payment will be made e.g. payment on acceptance or by day/month/year, whichever occurs soonest.

An example of this occurred when a manufacturer accepted an L/C where payment was in stages (a percentage with order, a percentage on shipment, and the final percentage on acceptance).

The goods were manufactured and shipped, and the L/C discounted (drawn against) accordingly. The goods were installed by the distributor, but then an internal problem occurred with the board of directors of the purchasing company and the official acceptance was never signed off. The products were fully installed and in full use at the location, but due to the absence of an acceptance certificate from the buyer, the final part of the L/C was never paid. Eventually the L/C expired and the monies were lost without any recourse to the purchaser. If the manufacturer had specified a deadline date of latest payment, they would have been able to discount the L/C completely.

Discrepancies

Within the L/C there is a field for the description of goods and services; the exact detail of what is being purchased. If there is any difference in what is stated in this field to the supplier's invoice, there will be discrepant documents and a possibility that the L/C will not be paid. This can be a difference in a single letter or number in any part of the invoice or Bill of Lading.

If it is a minor discrepancy, most banks will present the documents as discrepant and request payment anyway (which usually occurs); however extra bank charges will be incurred to accept discrepant documentation.

By far the easiest and cleanest solution is to ask the buyer to state "Goods / Services as per attached quotation number xxx, dated day/month/year". This should ensure that all part numbers, descriptions, services, prices, terms and conditions are as the quotation or pro forma and negate any problem with discrepancies.

Verify that your company name and bank details as beneficiary are correct on the L/C; even one incorrect letter can be an excuse to delay or refuse payment.

Shipment dates

Always check the latest product ship date and expiry date of the L/C. Some customers will try to force the supplier to ship an order sooner than specified lead-times by specifying dates that are unachievable.

This should not be accepted without amendment because if shipment occurs just after the latest ship date, or shipment is made within the timeframe but documents are not presented at the bank for completion of processing before the expiry date, the supplier will not be paid on the L/C.

The applicant (buyer) may be reluctant to open an L/C in the timeframe specified – as soon as the L/C is opened, the buyer's funds are frozen at the bank, which affects cash flow. The buyer may request that goods are manufactured prior to opening the L/C, which is then transferring the risk on to the manufacturer as they are then dependant on receiving the L/C before shipment, which in worst cases may never appear and the supplier could be left with a stock of finished goods.

Templates

The principal should work with their bank to formulate an L/C template, which shows each field number and the correct detail that should be completed to ensure the L/C is clean. This template can then be circulated to agents or distributors, and included with quotations to customers, to ensure that when an L/C is opened, it is compliant.

What does all this mean?

The exporter and buyer can agree detailed terms, as part of the commercial contract. This can include exactly what documents need to be produced and precisely what detail such documents should quote.

L/Cs, as well as offering a bank's commitment to pay, also offer benefits in terms of finance.

Standby Letters of Credit (SBLCs) or Bank Guarantees

SBLCs are similar to Bank Guarantees, in that they sit behind a transaction and are only called upon if the buyer fails to pay in the normal course of business (which is often Open Account). They can be particularly useful to cover an underlying financial risk where multiple payments are to be made, possibly as part of an agreed schedule. However, they do not offer the documentary control of L/Cs to buyers and, as such, they are an unconditional guarantee.

International Customer Risks

Can they / will the customer pay? Exporters should find out everything they can about their buyers. Banks can help by contacting the buyer's bank for a reference. There are many commercial organisations that can provide credit information at relatively little cost. The exporter may also use any local contacts or agents who might be prepared to find out the buyers status.

Other payment mechanisms

SWIFT Inter-Bank Transfer - now firmly established as standard practice in the major trading nations. The buyer will instruct their bank to make payment to any bank account specified by the exporter. It is good practice, therefore, for the exporter to include their account details on their invoice heads.

Buyer's Cheque: an unsatisfactory method of settlement for the exporter as it carries the risk of dishonour upon presentation as well as the added inconvenience of being slow to clear. There is also the very real danger of the cheque being lost in transit. A cheque is also unsatisfactory if it is in the currency of the buyer, as this will take longer to clear and will involve additional bank charges. Exporters should only use this method if they have an established trading history with their customer or in cases where the profit margin has been increased to offset cash flow problems anticipated by the delay in receiving payment.

Banker's Draft: this is arranged by the buyer who asks their bank to raise a draft on its corresponding bank in the exporter's country. Provides additional security to a buyer's cheque, but can be costly to arrange and run the risk of getting lost in transit.

International Money Orders: these are similar in nature to postal orders. They are pre-printed therefore cheaper to obtain than a Banker's Draft, although there is the risk of loss in transit.

Cost and Complexity

When selecting the payment mechanism, the cost and complexity must be taken into account; from the seller's perspective, the more secure the payment method, the more costly it will be to process and the more complex to manage for both parties.

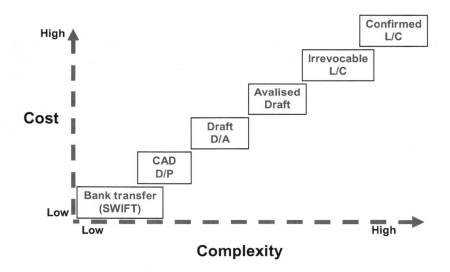

Using payment mechanisms can be a way of increasing business through helping the buyer pay for the products or services; the buyer may not be able to pay in advance, but may be able to pay at a later date. If the seller and the buyer can agree on a secure payment mechanism with terms that suit both sides, then the buyer may be able to place the order.

Using payment mechanisms to increase business takes an understanding of the mechanism and the costs and risks associated with it, knowledge of the buyer's country risk factor, the level and relationship between banks, export insurance and payment terms. The most important factor is to keep flexibility in mind and finding ways to reduce risk and exposure on both sides.

Third party collections

Factoring, Forfaiting, and Confirming

Factoring is the discounting of a foreign account receivable that does not involve a draft. The exporter transfers title of its foreign accounts receivable to a factoring house (an organisation that specialises in the financing of accounts receivable) for cash at a discount from the face value. Although factoring is sometimes done without recourse to the exporter (obligation for collection is not down to the exporter), the specific arrangements should be verified by the exporter.

Forfaiting is the selling, at a discount, of longer term accounts receivable or promissory notes of the foreign buyer. These instruments may also carry the guarantee of the foreign government. Because forfaiting may be done either with or without recourse to the exporter, the specific arrangements should be verified by the exporter.

Confirming is a financial service undertaken by an independent company which confirms an export order in the seller's country and makes payment for the goods in the currency of that country. Among the items eligible for confirmation (and thereby eligible for credit terms) are the goods themselves; inland, air, and ocean transportation costs; forwarding fees; custom brokerage fees and duties. For the exporter, confirming means that the entire export transaction from plant to end user can be fully coordinated and paid for over time.

Third party collections can make a substantial difference to cash flow but they do incur costs which will impact the supplier's profitability.

Some international buyers will respect the demands from a factoring or forfaiting company more than from the supplier. However, most customers who receive a factored or forfaited invoice will suspect that the principal has financial difficulties. Culturally it could be seen as an insult as the buyer will think they are not trusted to pay.

Third party collection companies do not normally have the same concerns regarding the future business of the supplier; they will use legalities and push hard until payment is received. This can have a negative effect on the business moving forwards as the agent, distributor or final customer will not enjoy dealing with these companies, and could decide not to deal with the principal as a result.

The larger collection companies usually have international departments where local language speakers chase payment by phone and mail, which improves communication and speed of receipt.

Many banks have their own in-house collections service, and may try to encourage the small business owner to forfait or factor their invoices to aid cash flow.

The small business owner should take a long term view on any collection services and evaluate the impact on the business over the long term. Once the services of a third party collection company have been used, it is very easy to become reliant on the company, which can be to the detriment of the business relationship and development.

Export Credit Insurance

Most financial institutions will advocate the use of Export Insurance; whereby the international debt is insured by the supplier against non-collection. These policies can be expensive to put in place, but if there is a high level of receivable invoices in a particular country, it may be advantageous to cover all eventualities.

Export credit insurance policies have specific country limits of cover, which the insurer will advise. This type of insurance would mainly cover Open Account transactions or non-guaranteed transactions, not an Irrevocable L/C or any other guaranteed payment term.

The terms of export insurance policies usually have an excess; if a claim is made, the claimant (the policy holder) is responsible for a threshold amount, the insurance company pays the balance from that threshold to the limit of the policy.

Exporter managers should be aware of the limitations of using this type of insurance and verify with their financial controller/advisor before entering into business negotiations whether the target country poses too much of a risk. Some financial managers will not conduct business which is in excess of the country credit insurance limit.

Insurance is another mechanism to aid growth in international business, not a policy that is used to limit the value of product or service supplied.

The Five Deal Breakers in International Trade

When conducting an international deal, the seller must understand the five "deal breakers":

- Payment terms
- Payment mechanism
- Incoterm (products only)
- Bank and relationships
- Currency and foreign exchange (FX) rate

These five "deal breakers" must be understood because:
- They can completely eliminate all profit from the sale as each one carries a risk and an exposure to costs that can be out of the seller's control.
- They affect the control and risk during shipment of goods.

The Effects on Profit

Payment Terms:
Whether the payment is in advance, or is a usance term (e.g. 30 day payment terms), the delay in receiving payment will impact the exporter's cash flow, and can also carry costs. The costs can be through having to "finance" the manufacturing process or the service, lack of bank interest, having to borrow money in order to bridge the debt or discounting the invoice (forfaiting).

Payment Mechanism:

International payment mechanisms incur bank costs; even a simple electronic transfer will carry a cost to the accounts being debited and credited. The more complicated the payment mechanism, the more expensive the charges. If a payment mechanism is used which can require amendments (i.e. an L/C), each amendment will carry an extra charge, as will confirmation or any aval.

These charges can also be applied to the beneficiaries or the applicant's account, or shared between the two parties. If the responsibility for charges is not agreed in advance, the exporter could find that the payment received has had all charges covering the payment mechanism (both the buyer and the sellers) debited at source.

Incoterm:

The shipping/delivery obligation of the exporter will be determined by the Incoterm negotiated. If the exporter knows the costs for shipment/delivery, these costs will be built into the pricing. However, the costs are out of the control of the exporter and if the costs change for any reason the exporter incurs the exposure to the variation. Negotiating an ex-works (Incoterms 2000) deal means that the exporter can be responsible for items within his control, and mitigate any exposure on any shipment charge changes. The shipment/delivery charges should be dealt with as a separate line item.

Bank and Relationships:

Where a direct communication channel is in place between banks, they are said to be correspondent banks. Not all banks have direct relationships which means that payments are sent or received through an intermediary bank. This extra step in the process incurs extra costs, which must be understood and accounted for.

Most banks in the first-world are known as first class banks. Banks in the second and third world may not be at the level of first-class banks, and may not be able to process or guarantee payments. The exporter should know the names of the first-class banks in the destination country and insist that only one of these banks is used, and one that preferably has a direct correspondent relationship with their own bank.

Currency and Foreign Exchange (FX) Rate:

The currency of the transaction must be clearly defined. If the buyer sends payments in a foreign currency to the exporter's bank, the payment can incur negotiation charges from the bank when the currency is transferred into that account.

If the exporter agrees to receive payment in another currency, all fluctuation risk on the foreign currency amount is borne by the exporter. In regions where two currencies are tied (e.g. UK and Euro), fluctuation may be a minimal percentage which can be built into the pricing. However, in other regions where the currency floats through open trading, the exporter may wish to speak to a foreign exchange specialist and hedge or forward buy the currency.

Understanding the "deal breakers" is all about minimising risk and impact due to variation and exposure. The exporter must know the costs associated with each of the elements and how any single change in one of these commercial costs can impact the sale as a whole, and the compound effect of multiple changes of multiple items.

The Effects on Risk and Control of Shipment of Goods

One of the most frequently asked questions is "which Incoterm should I use?".

The reality is that this is not a question that can be answered simply. The Incoterm must relate to the payment term, payment mechanism and insurance of the shipment.

Only two Incoterms specify when insurance is to be bought and issued: CIP and CIF, and if neither of these terms is used, then the payment term and mechanism must be taken in to account.

For example, if you have an ex-works Incoterm and payment is with order, the buyer is responsible for shipment and therefore it is their decision on whether to insure the shipment. However, if the Incoterm used is CPT (carriage paid to...) and the payment term is on delivery, then the seller has an obligation to ensure that the goods arrive at the destination in order to be paid. If for some reason the shipment does not arrive and is not insured, then the seller bears all of the exposure and costs in replacing the shipment.

These issues are also impacted by payment mechanism. Using an example of payment by Letter of Credit (L/C) and payment term on delivery at the premises (DDU – Delivered Duty Unpaid...). If the goods are delayed during shipment for some reason, the terms of the L/C may expire before the delivery takes place, then in this case the goods may arrive but the seller would not be able to be paid by L/C; the seller would insure against such an eventuality.

When looking at risk and control, the seller must understand the level of exposure, and whether there is a risk that must be insured against. The deal breakers must be formulated to ensure that the seller retains control of the goods and/or shipment to guarantee that they will be paid and the transaction not lost even though the products have been produced and shipped.

References

The following references were used in compiling information detailed in this book.

- Buying or Selling? Negotiating for Profit.   © Gary Jennings 2007
- International Marketing Plans.   © Gary Jennings 2007
- Michael E. Porter, Competitive Strategy: *Techniques for Analysing Industries and Competitors*, The Free Press, 1980.
- Tools for Success, Dr S Turner (2002)
- ICC Guide to Incoterms 2000, Professor Jan Ramberg
- SITPRO Ltd www.sitpro.org.uk
- The ICC Short Form Model Contracts ICC Publication No. 634 E Copyright © 2001 – International Chamber of Commerce (ICC), Paris. The competition rules for supply and distribution agreements © European Communities 2000.
- Introduction to Engaging Commercial Agents and the EU Agents Directive. © Mette Lorentzen, Euro Info Centre, London Chamber of Commerce and Industry, November 2004, Update February 2006

Index